NORTH NORFOLK
AROUND BLAKENEY, CLEY and HOLT

JOHN CURTIS

Text by Richard Ashby

SALMON

INTRODUCTION

The little coastal towns of North Norfolk were once thriving ports and Blakeney traded along the east coast of England and across the North Sea as far as the Baltic while Cley was once of greater importance than Kings Lynn. Fishing was important too and nearby there were salt pans which provided the salt to preserve the fish in the days before refrigeration. So much was required that local ships had to go as far as Spain to obtain sufficient.

It was the shifting sands and shingle which created Blakeney Point but at the same time destroyed the town's sea-going trade as the creek silted up. But man's interventions have been disastrous too and the reclaiming of the marshes for agriculture caused unforeseen damage to the harbours.

Salthouse from Salthouse Heath

As a result, nothing remains of the bustling tidal quays of the once thriving twin ports of Cley and Wiveton, a mile or so inland, except the great churches either side of the little River Glaven. Away from the sea is a landscape of gently rolling farmland. There are quiet villages and the busy country town of Holt. Once there were many mills, powered either by water or wind, for grain was the main produce of this fertile soil. Now it is tourism which sustains the local economy. Visitors come to walk and to sail, to watch birds and seals on the extensive mud flats and nature reserves and to enjoy the quiet beauties of this lovely and peaceful corner of Norfolk where the low hills and the vast expanses of the salt marshes meet the wide, blue Norfolk sky.

Blakeney Quay

The name 'Blakeney' comes from the Anglo-Saxon and means 'Black Island'. It is first mentioned in the Domesday Book of 1086 and it has long been a thriving port, trading all over Europe in grain and wool. The local fishing industry was once a thriving business with the fishing boats going as far north as Iceland.

The Creek, Blakeney

By the early 15th century Blakeney was listed as one of the few ports permitted to trade in horses, gold and silver. Pilgrims were also important, both those travelling to Walsingham nearby and those leaving for the shrine of St James at Compestella in Spain. In Elizabethan times Blakeney was required to send three ships to help in the defeat of the Spanish Armada and imports included children's toys from Hamburg, raisins and spices from the East and wine. In the mid 19th century there were regular packet boats to Hull and London. The coastal trade continued well into the 20th century with coal coming into the little port but the silting up of the harbour eventually became so bad that this trade too ceased and it is leisure sailing which now dominates the quay and surrounding creeks.

Old cottages at Blakeney
The predominant local building materials of brick and flint give the village its characteristic appearance. The clay for the brick is found all around. Pebbles are formed by the action of the sea pounding the flints it has scoured from the cliffs further east.

Blakeney from the Creek
At low tide the quay at Blakeney is effectively cut off from the sea as far as boats are concerned. In 1817 an attempt was made to halt the decline of the port by cutting a new channel to the sea but this reprieve was short lived.

High Street, Blakeney

The main business of Blakeney today, as before, takes place around Blakeney Haven, which is the centre of the sailing and other leisure activities. It is overlooked by the large Blakeney Hotel and the granaries and warehouses, which are the lasting reminders of Blakeney's former trade. When the quayside is particularly busy, it is pleasant to turn aside from this bustle into the quieter High Street, which rises gently from the quay side towards the parish church, set a little way inland. It is lined with attractive 18th and early 19th century houses, mostly of brick and flint, although some are rendered and white or colour-washed.

The Guildhall, Blakeney

This impressive vaulted room of brick arches resting on stone pillars may have been the undercroft of the Guildhall of Blakeney's fish merchants. Alternatively, it may have been a store room for an important merchant and used as a warehouse for his trade. Little of the structure above, built of Flemish brick, remains.

Blakeney Point

The sea continuously erodes the cliffs of north-eastern Norfolk and the currents transport the eroded material westwards and deposit it off the coast. At Blakeney a great spit has been formed of sand and shingle, behind which have developed sand banks, salt marshes and Blakeney Harbour itself, with a wide sheet of water at high tide but a network of creeks and channels at low tide. The mud flats, salt marshes and dunes are home to a great variety of birds, which breed here or pass through on their annual migration, as well as the famous seal sanctuary.

Church of St Nicholas, Blakeney

Blakeney church is unusual in having two towers, the smaller one having been a 'beacon' tower, in which a light was placed at night as a guide to shipping. The two towers together may also have formed 'leading lights' which, when lined up, would enable vessels to find the safe way through the channel in and out of the harbour.

Newgate Green, Cley next the Sea
This was the heart of the old port of Cley. Until the middle of the 17th century the River Glaver was tidal to here and was lined on both sides with busy wharves. The grand church reflects the wealth and importance of the little port which grew up around it.

High Street, Cley next the Sea
After a great fire in 1612 the village was rebuilt further north and many lovely and historic buildings survive from the following centuries; 'Rocket House' in the High Street contained the coastguard station and housed the rocket-propelled life saving apparatus.

An Old Corner, Cley next the Sea
It is difficult to believe that this little place was once greater than Kings Lynn. By the Middle Ages Cley (pronounced Cly) was a flourishing port and in medieval time the quays stretched inland along both banks of the River Glaven as far as the church. The great fire of 1612 destroyed 117 houses and the village was rebuilt further north, since the reclamation of the marshes was already affecting the tides in the estuary with its consequent silting up. By the mid 17th century the estuary was no longer navigable. Today, Cley is a pretty place of flint and brick houses, which show the influence of the trade with the Netherlands in their Dutch gables.

The Mill, Cley next the Sea
The windmill in its prominent position is a well known landmark and something of an icon for the village. It dates from 1850, but stopped working at the end of the First World War and was converted into a holiday home in 1921.

Church of St Nicholas, Salthouse

Salthouse was also once a port and, as its name implies, was a centre for the salt pans in which sea water was evaporated to produce the ingredients necessary to preserve fish. The scratchings on the back of the seats in the church were, no doubt, done by bored choirboys to whom these ships would have been a familiar sight.

Church of St Mary, Wiveton

North Norfolk has many wonderful churches which seem to us to be much larger than necessary for the population they were built to serve. We have to remember that the churches had important social as well as religious functions, and they reflect the prosperity of the medieval 'age of faith'.

Weybourne Beach

Sheringham cliffs give way to lower lying land at Weybourne and a great shingle bank protects the marshes and the village from the sea. Because it is one of the few places along the coast where deep water vessels can come close to the shore, it has always been feared that the area, known as 'Weybourne Hope', was vulnerable to invasion. It is believed that the Angles and the Danes landed here more than once during the so-called Dark Ages; the area was fortified against the threat from the Armada, during Napoleonic times, and again in the two World Wars. An old saying has it that:-

'He who would old England win
Must at Weybourne Hope begin'.

Weybourne Mill

Windmills are an important feature of the North Norfolk landscape and were essential for the grinding of locally-produced grain. This one dates from 1850 and is a 'tower mill' with a brick-built tower and a 'cap' which turned to enable the sails to face the wind direction. It is unusual in having the miller's house directly attached.

Priory and Church of All Saints, Weybourne
Early in the 13th century Augustinian canons
built a priory in Weybourne on the site of an
earlier Saxon church, incorporating some of
the earlier building, including the impressive
central tower. The monastic buildings are
now in ruins but the church itself, which
had become quite decrepit over the centuries,
was restored in the 19th century.

Holt

A few miles inland up the Glaver Valley,
the town of Holt was originally centred
around the impressive church. Following
a disastrous fire in 1708 the centre of
the town was rebuilt around the Market
Place, where many 18th century
buildings remain. Sir John Gresham,
a Lord Mayor of London, was a native
of the town and in 1562 gave the town
its grammar school, which he established
in his house in the Market Place.
Its replacement of 1858 is still there
with the arms of Sir John and the
Fishmongers' Company (of which
Sir John was the master) over the door.
The school became a fine public school
in 1900 and has moved to newer
buildings on the edge of the town.

Church of St Andrew the Apostle, Holt

The original 14th century church was largely gutted in the great fire of 1708. The thatched chancel was burned out, the lead in the windows melted and the steeple was destroyed, though the arches and windows survived. It was restored in 1727 and again, much more grandly, between 1862 and 1874 by William Butterfield, the well-known Victorian architect.

Memorial Cross, Market Place, Holt

Holt has a long history. It is listed in the Domesday Book as having its own market and its own port at Cley on the coast. The town retains something of an old-world air of former times with its small shops and narrow backstreets, including 'Fish Hill', the site of the old fish market.

Letheringsett Mill

There has been a mill at Letheringsett, on the outskirts of Holt, since at least the time of the Domesday book. The present building dates from 1802 and has been in constant use since that time. A great restoration has taken place in the years since 1987, including new floors and a new roof and major work to the machinery. The flour, which is produced from locally grown grain, sells across the world.

The River Glaven, Glandford

For many centuries the tides came up the River Glaven and across this ford to Bayfield, another half mile further on. Bayfield Hall was the home of Sir Alfred Joddrell, who built the model village of Glandford. In the grounds of the church is his Dutch-gabled museum, opened in 1915, to house his collection of shells from around the world.

Morston Quay

In the early part of the 18th century Daniel Defoe wrote in his *Tour through the Whole Island of Great Britain* 'at Morston, the art of smuggling was so much in practice'. Boats leave from the little quay here taking visitors to see the seals off Blakeney Point.

Church of All Saints, Morston

The village church is set on a slight rise just on the edge of the village and there are fine views of the marshes and over towards Blakeney. Lesser known than some others, the church has much of interest especially the painted panels, which remarkably survived the Reformation.

Binham Priory

Only a fragment of the original church at Binham remains, but what is left is impressive enough. The great west front with its now-blocked window gives an idea of the scale of the whole. The nave of the priory church was used by the local people as their parish church and this survived after the Dissolution of the Monasteries.

Church of St John the Baptist, Stiffkey

It is impossible to separate this church from the story of the Vicar, the Reverend Harold Davidson, who reputedly brought back London prostitutes to his vicarage.

The parish was little bothered by the singular behaviour, but it disturbed the Bishop, who had the vicar 'defrocked'.

He died several years later after being mauled by a lion and was buried back at Stiffkey, where his grave is still cared for.

The Quay, Wells-next-the-Sea
The little town of Wells, once an important harbour, was founded where the streams flowing from under the chalk provided easy access to water. Wells makes its claim to be near the sea in its name, but the sea has receded over the centuries and it is now a long mile from the quay to the sea itself. Once busy with shipping from along the coast and trading with northern Europe, the harbour is now almost entirely given over to pleasure boating although there are reminders of the mercantile past in the granaries and warehouses, which have now been put to other uses.

Common Place, Little Walsingham
The two open spaces of this pilgrimage village, Common Place and Friday Market, each have a pre-Reformation hostelry. In the centre of Common Place is a conduit which brought water to the town. It once housed a small lock-up and on the roof is a brazier, lit at times of celebration.

Holkham Hall

Thomas Coke, Earl of Leicester, together with Lord Burlington and William Kent, created Holkham Hall over a twenty-five year period, from 1734 to 1759, and filled its magnificent Palladian interior, with books and works of art collected on his Grand Tour. The Hall sits in extensive parkland and is, justifiably, the principal tourist attraction in the area.

Published and Printed in Great Britain by
J. Salmon Ltd., Sevenoaks, Kent TN13 1BB. © 2007
Website: www.jsalmon.com. Telephone: 01732 452381. Email: enquiries@jsalmon.co.uk.

Design by John Curtis. Text and photographs © John Curtis.
Photographs pages twenty-four and thirty-two by kind permission of Letheringsett Mill and Holkham Hall.

ISBN 1-84640-099-6
Title page photograph: Blakeney Quay   Front cover photograph: Blakeney   Back cover photograph: Cley next the Sea.

Salmon Books
ENGLISH IMAGES SERIES
Photography by John Curtis

Titles available in this series

English Abbeys and Priories

English Gardens

English Country Towns

English Cottages

English Landscape Gardens

English Follies

English Villages

English Country Pubs

English Castles

English Cathedrals

English Country Churches

Jane Austen's England

Romantic England

Mysterious England